P9-BXW-113

ALASKA'S
BUSH PLANES

Text by Ned Rozell
Foreword by Harmon "Bud" Helmericks

ALASKA NORTHWEST BOOKS®
Anchorage • Portland

Barrow•

Prudhoe
Bay■

Beaufor
Sea

THE ARCTIC

Arctic Ocean

Russia

ARCTIC CIRCLE

Colville River

Noatak River

BROOKS RANGE

ALASKA

Kotzebue•

*Kotzebue
Sound*

■ Prospect
Creek

Porcupine River

Fort
Yukon•

*Gulf of
Anadyr*

Strait

SEWARD PENINSULA

Koyukuk River

Yukon River

Tanana•

INTERIOR

•Fairbanks

Bering

Nome•

Tanana

Norton Sound

River

MILES
0   100   200

Yukon River

Innoko River

Mount
McKinley▲

RANGE

Susitna River

WRA
MOUN

N
W   E
S

**WESTERN
ALASKA**

•McGrath

ALASKA RANGE

•Talkeetna

KUSKOKWIM MTNS

SOUTHCENTRAL

Valdez•

Cop
Ri

Kuskokwim River

Anchorage●

•Cordo

Bering Sea

Bethel•

**KENAI
PENINSULA**

Cook Inlet

*Iliamna
Lake*

*Kuskokwim
Bay*

Dillingham•

*Gulf
of
Alaska*

MILES
0   100   200

*Bristol
Bay*

•Kodiak

N
W   E
S

Aleutian Islands

Kodiak
Island

CONTINUED ON
INSET ABOVE

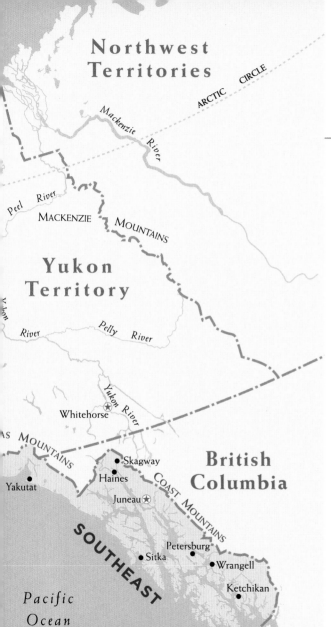

Table of Contents

FOREWORD

Those Who Flew

I once flew two old Eskimos to a small lake on the north side of the Brooks Range, to a spot where the "Old People" said there was gold. Here they wanted to be left to spend the summer. There wasn't any lake on the sketchy map I had, so we squatted on a sandbar while Old Harry drew us a map in the sand. He had walked there with his grandfather forty years ago. I hadn't seen the lake, but I had a general idea of the area about three hundred miles away, so I flew until I came to a branch of the Nanushuk River, where Harry took over the navigating, saying "Take that branch," then a few minutes later, "Go over that ridge, fly to that hill." After a half hour, he said, "The lake is behind that ridge."

Never once had he hesitated, and when we topped the ridge, there was the lake exactly as he had drawn it. Yet it had been forty years since he had walked there as a teenage boy, using pack dogs.

I left them there in that Arctic mountain fastness. In our Cessna 170B floatplane I had taken them where they wanted to be in hours. Forty years earlier, way before airplanes, it had taken months. What hadn't changed: they would use their same system of living through two No. 1 traps to catch parka squirrels and a .22 rifle to get a caribou for food.

I was back two weeks later and there was a note by the rock where they had unloaded: "No gold. Having a fine time. We will walk to Negilik [the spot on the Arctic Ocean where our home is] see you in the fall."

They had lived on parka squirrels and caribou. They had three large rivers to cross and each time they made a little boat out of willow branches and covered it with caribou hide. They hadn't found any gold, and I believe they hadn't even looked. The gold they sought was in being where they wanted to be and in doing what they wanted to do. You must really love a land to recall every tiny detail of a trip you made decades ago.

This was true of we old-time Bush pilots. We loved the land, all of its inhabitants, and especially the people we served. And we really loved our airplanes.

In my years of flying Alaska, which began in about 1945, airplanes went through many changes, and at one time there were more than one hundred manufacturers.

Lowell Thomas Jr. flies his Helio Courier in Denali Park's Ruth Amphitheater on a flight to pick up skiers. The Helio Courier is unique for its leading-edge slats, which drop forward as the plane nears stalling speed, giving the plane more lift and allowing flight at slower speeds.

People in Alaska needed more and more service by air and the pilots were adapting airplanes to serve them, even tying things on the outside. Aircraft manufacturers cooperated with the explorers and Bush pilots to build the sort of airplanes needed. There were Cubs, Taylorcrafts, the Bellanca Skyrocket, Cessnas, Stinsons, Beechcraft, and even the DC-3, C-46, and later the Hercules pressed into Bush service.

The single-engine airplanes like the Cub, the Cessna 170 or '80 were really the favorites, especially for winter flying. They were easier to heat in the dark of early morning and easier to put "to bed" in the cold fading light of evening. You took care of them as if your life depended upon them because in truth, it did.

An old prospector once told me that there were only two kinds of people in the world, those who flew and those who wished they could. It is likely true today.

I still look up when I hear a plane.

—HARMON "BUD" HELMERICKS
Author of *The Last of the Bush Pilots*, and 10 other books
Fairbanks, Alaska, 2003

INTRODUCTION

Frontier Flight in the 21st Century   by Ned Rozell

From my home in Fairbanks, I sometimes hear the rattle of a Piper Super Cub as it climbs north. I look up and see the plane's balloon tires floating above the spruce trees and wonder where those tires will next spin— through the polished rock and clear water of the upper Canning River, on the gravel airstrip at Anaktuvuk Pass beneath pointy white peaks of the Brooks Range, or maybe a field of lichen and rock on a lonely hilltop in the Fortymile Country. As the Cub's engine fades to silence, I imagine the pilot standing in a place few people ever get to experience.

Alaska has changed in many ways since the first aircraft visited the state in 1913, but one feature has remained the same—Bush planes are the best way to access this vast, ungroomed land. Alaska stretches from north to south the distance from Boston to Miami, and east to west the equivalent of Washington, D.C., to Salt Lake City. Cars and trucks enable Alaskans to sample a well-trodden grid of pavement and gravel in the Interior, Southcentral, and to a lesser extent, the Arctic, but Alaska has fewer miles of road than Vermont. Boats navigating Alaska's coastline or big rivers plying its interior arteries offer another way to of reach Alaska's backcountry, but mountains, glaciers, tundra bogs, rainforest jungles and the limits of the human mind and body discourage further penetration into Alaska's 365 million acres.

When in 1903 Wilber and Orville Wright succeeded in getting a heavier-than-air vehicle off the ground in North Carolina, they invented a device that seemed custom-made for Alaska. Ten years later, the first airplane to reach Alaska made its way to the territory packed in a wooden crate that traveled by steamship and paddle wheeler from Seattle to Skagway to Whitehorse to Tanana to Fairbanks. During an exhibition flight on the outskirts of town on July 4, 1913, entrepreneur and pilot James Martin circled his biplane over muskeg and boreal forest for nine minutes. The hundreds of Alaskans watching from rooftops and woodpiles saw the state's future banking overhead at 70 miles per hour.

Billy Mitchell, an adventurer who learned the boggy and buggy reality of ground travel in the territory while helping string a telegraph wire from Valdez to Eagle in

Wien Alaska Airways delivered the mail from Weeks Field in Fairbanks, circa 1929. At right is a Fokker, the forerunner of the Ford Tri-Motor. At left is a Stinson Detroiter, one of two used in the famed Wilkins Expedition in 1927.

1903, promoted the second appearance of aircraft in Alaska in 1920. Four Army de Havilland biplanes flew from New York to Nome and back.

At the time the de Havillands roared over Alaska's quiet forests and mountains, Alaskans in the Bush received their U.S. mail by boat in the summer and dog team after the rivers froze. That began to change in February 1924, when a schoolteacher pilot named Carl Ben Eielson flew 164 pounds of mail from Fairbanks to McGrath and returned intact on the same day.

Eielson, flying in an open-cockpit de Havilland DH-4 biplane, waved with his bearskin mittens as he passed over a dog musher named Fred Milligan, who had carried mail by dog sled for more than 20 years. Milligan was mushing on the cold flats between the Kuskokwim Mountains and the Alaska Range.

"I decided then and there that Alaska was no country for dogs," Milligan told Jean Potter, author of *The Flying North*. The musher later took a job with Pan American Airways.

The skies over Alaska soon hummed with activity.

Among the many feats that Joe Crosson squeezed into 15 years of flying in Alaska was his hurdling of Mount McKinley in 1931, when he fixed its approximate elevation of 20,000 feet with his altimeter; Crosson later became the first pilot to land on the mountain, in 1932 ferrying climbers and equipment onto the Muldrow Glacier with a Fairchild 71 on skis. The trip, in support of a mission to set up a cosmic ray observatory on Mount McKinley, also marked the first aircraft support of scientists in Alaska, now a daily practice in summer.

Crosson's friend Noel Wien was the first to fly from Anchorage to Fairbanks, making the trip in 3 hours, 45 minutes in 1924 by following the railroad track north in a de Havilland biplane. By the late 1930s, Fairbanks had 3,000 people and about 50 airplanes, a ratio far above most towns in the Lower 48 states and one of the highest in the world.

Small planes are still the number-one choice of Alaskans who want or need to reach remote villages, coastal towns, or "off airstrip" gravel bars or hilltops. Though Alaska's population has increased tenfold since the first plane appeared, it is still the only state in which residents can't jump in the car and drive to the capital.

Live in Alaska for more than one year, and you will know at least one pilot. According to statistics from the Federal Aviation Administration, as of January 2001, there were 8,053 registered aircraft in Alaska and 10,016 Alaskans with a pilot's license. When you divide that into the state's 626,932 residents, one out of 63 people here have the ability to fly and a certificate to back it up. More than half of those pilots live in Southcentral Alaska; the rest are scattered to the farthest corners of the state.

Alaskans favor single- and twin-engine planes fit with landing gear that suits the landscape—floats are a favorite for salt-water landings in Southeast and for the millions of lakes throughout the state. While straight skis are a favorite after the snow flies, pilots also use ski/wheel combinations when taking off from gravel or paved airstrips and landing on glaciers high in the mountains. Thirty-inch tundra tires are a favorite of pilots who bounce to a landing on gravel bars, alpine hilltops, and other improvised airstrips. Amphibious planes, such as the Grumman Goose, give pilots the option to land either belly-down in water or on land with the help of retractable gear. Pilots who land on tundra and gravel bars prefer "tail dragger," aircraft with a pivoting wheel under the tail.

"Nose-wheel" planes are often limited to improved airstrips because their propellers are more vulnerable to dipping down into gravel or other obstructions upon landing.

Pilots of Alaska's small planes carry mail, groceries, and passengers to Bush villages and ferry hikers, hunters, and fishermen to some of the prime spots in North America. They often need to carry items that don't fit in the airplane, such as canoes that ride like lampreys on the bellies of planes, or 60-inch moose antlers tied to struts.

Pilots sometimes modify their aircraft to help them do their jobs. Wildlife biologists at the Alaska Department of Fish and Game attach radio-tracking antennas to the wing struts of their agency's Bellanca Scouts to track sheep, moose, and wolves; a glaciologist at the University of Alaska installed a laser-altimetry system in the belly of his Super Cub so he can measure the precise height of glaciers. Other pilots use planes to get a seagull's view for commercial fishermen, spotting fish from the air, and many tourists are getting their most memorable views of Alaska from the seats of small aircraft.

Pilots face occasional crummy weather all over the state, from the thick fogs where the warm waters of the Japanese current meet the cold Bering Sea to the dense, frigid air over the Interior, where a thermometer at Prospect Creek once dropped to 80 below. Add to the mix the zero hours of direct sunshine north of the Arctic Circle in January or the sudden winds that whip up ground blizzards on the western coast, and Alaska pilots face some of the most varied flying conditions on the continent.

Many of Alaska's most experienced pilots fly for a living as air-taxi pilots or carrying mail and passengers on short hops between villages. Pilots in Talkeetna make thousands of flights to Mount McKinley's Kahiltna Glacier, ferrying tons of gear, food and climbers attempting North America's highest peak or the other impressive mountains that surround it. Southeast pilots flying turbo Super Otters use the planes' power to carry more than one ton of cargo to remote bays popular with hunters, fishermen, climbers, and scientists. Workhorse Piper Cherokees deliver mail and passengers throughout the expanse of Alaska's Interior, which is larger than some Lower 48 states.

In a scenario somewhat unique to Alaska, pilots in the urban centers of Anchorage, Fairbanks, and Juneau often change clothes on Friday afternoons before jumping into their Maules, Citabrias, and Cessnas and heading for quiet country. Many of those planes are older than the men and women who fly them. A typical Piper Super Cub—perhaps Alaska's most popular Bush plane—came off the assembly line in the 1950s. Most of Alaska's beloved small planes have had their fabric skin replaced several times and their engines rebuilt almost as often. Because many Bush planes, such as the sleek Helio Courier, have gone out of production, pilots often have trouble finding parts; resourceful mechanics are often the best friends of the Alaska Bush pilot.

The enduring usefulness of Bush planes says a lot about the people who fly them, and it says even more about Alaska, which has remained in effect roadless since it became a state in 1959. With much of the state either too rugged or too politically protected for the construction of new roads, Bush planes will buzz the skies over Alaska for many years to come.

A Beaver DHC-2 prepares to take off from McKinley Park's rugged airstrip in 1952. This Beaver was a military model, one of the first to be manufactured. At center are two Stinson Voyagers, and at right is a Taylorcraft BC1ZD.

THE INTERIOR

The Interior is an Iowa-size region of boreal forest and muskeg lowlands spreading between the Alaska Range and the Brooks Range. Its distance from the sea makes the Interior Alaska's hottest place in the summer (the all-time high of 100° F was measured at Fort Yukon) and also the state's coldest place (the all-time low of 80 below zero occurred at Prospect Creek off the Dalton Highway).

The extreme cold of the region is a unique challenge. Pilots flying at temperatures lower than minus 10° F must preheat their engines before flying. A favorite method of one Super Cub pilot is to fire up a couple of camp stoves, and then cover the flames with stovepipes that extend into the engine compartment. Through trial and error, pilots using this method learn how much heat they can apply without melting wire bundles inside.

Despite its extremes, Interior Alaska features some of the most stable flying conditions in Alaska and dry conditions for most of the year, except in August, when the Interior receives much of its yearly precipitation due to a shift in the jet stream that forces moist air northeast between the Kuskokwim Mountains and the Alaska Range.

A tricycle-gear Cessna 206 takes off from the frozen Yukon River at Ruby. The downward-curved wingtips are a modification that provides extra lift, allowing for slower-speed landings and takeoffs.

*T*wo 1941 trips I made to Fairbanks from Nome, both with a Gullwing Stinson, were especially memorable. One flight was with an engine that was missing badly. I was flying without freight or passengers. "You want me to fly that thing to Fairbanks [530 miles] with a bum engine?" I asked the mechanics, incredulous.

"We know what's wrong with it," they said. "It won't stop. We promise."

—RUDY BILLBERG as told to JIM REARDEN
In the Shadow of Eagles, 1992

New transportation meets old as pilot Paul Claus of Ultima Thule Lodge flies his 1,000-horsepower modified turbine Otter over Iditarod musher Martin Buser on the Yukon River near Ruby in the 2003 race.

A Piper Super Cub banks over the trans-Alaska pipeline on Alaska's North Slope. The 800-mile pipeline, which extends from Prudhoe Bay to Valdez, is easy to spot from the air.

Tourists on the sternwheeler *Discovery* in Fairbanks watch
a "short takeoff and landing," or STOL, demonstration by a
Piper Super Cub pilot. Many Alaska aircraft have modifications
that allow takeoff and landings from small landing strips.

Anchorage pilot Bill Kramer flies his Cessna 185 up Ruth Glacier near Mount McKinley on a sight-seeing trip. The 185 is one of the most popular aircraft in Alaska.

Two Super Cubs wait on a tundra strip near the Swift River
east of McGrath during hunting season. Bush planes allow
quick access to areas that would take days to reach on foot.

Floatplanes line the banks of the Chena River in Fairbanks next to a private gravel airstrip.

Planes of all shapes and sizes clutter the tarmac at Fairbanks International Airport. Pictured are a Piper Cherokee (low-wing design), and planes manufactured by Aeronca, Maule, and Cessna.

This Piper Super Cub nosed in while landing in drifted snow on tires. A mechanic repaired the plane to the point that its pilot was able to fly back to Anchorage.

Pilot/guide Jim Harrower takes off in a single-engine de Havilland Otter from a tundra strip in the Alaska Range. English aviation pioneer Geoffrey de Havilland built his first flying machine in 1909, and 50 aircraft have carried the de Havilland name since then. The company later produced some of the world's finest seaplanes.

A de Havilland Beaver from Trail Ridge Air picks up hunters from Eberhard Brunner's lodge near the Revelation Mountains in the Alaska Range. The Beaver has so much cargo space that transporting washing machines and other backcountry luxuries is no problem.

SOUTHEAST

The Southeast panhandle, extending for about 500 miles from Malaspina Glacier to the southern tip of Prince of Wales Island, is Alaska's wettest region, with up to 200 inches of precipitation each year. While sparse in roads, Southeast is lavish in rainforest spruce, hemlock, and cedar, fiords, the largest icefields in North America, and thousands of islands.

Floats are a favorite landing gear in Southeast, where rugged coastline and hills limit the availability of airstrips. Pilots in Southeast encounter some of the cloudiest weather in Alaska outside the Aleutians, and floats enable ocean landings in times of trouble or as a routine method of hopping from town to town.

Pilots landing on the region's many glaciers prefer wheel/skis, which enable travel from downtown Juneau to the magnificent ice fields nearby in minutes. The mountains of the Saint Elias, Fairweather, and Coast ranges often discourage flights inland because of the clouds stacked around them.

Navigation can also be a challenge for pilots new to the area because of the many fiords and islands that resemble one another.

From left to right, a de Havilland Otter, Cessna 206, and de Havilland Beaver on floats sit in the Juneau International Airport float pond with Mendenhall Glacier in the background. These planes belong to Wings of Alaska, a company that specializes in flightseeing trips.

Jeff Carlin of Juneau-based Carlin Air takes off in his de Havilland Beaver, "One Papa Mike," from Revillagigedo Channel near Bold Island in Southeast. Because of its large payload and ability for short takeoffs, some pilots call the Beaver a "glorified Super Cub."

A 450-horsepower 1959 de Havilland Beaver taxis across the dark waters of Punchbowl Lake in Misty Fjords National Monument.

*W*ith the arrival of the Pilgrim, Barr tried to establish regular service between Atlin and Juneau and he memorized the hundred-mile ice-capped route. First he had to overcome a big obstacle on flights to Juneau; he had no landing field.

—DERMOT COLE

Frank Barr: Bush Pilot in Alaska and the Yukon, 1986

A de Havilland Beaver carries tourists from Ketchikan over Punchbowl Lake in Misty Fjords National Monument during a three-hour flightseeing trip.

A de Havilland Twin Otter stops in Misty Fjords National Monument's Rudyerd Bay. This powerful aircraft has twin 680-horsepower turbine motors that allow a climb rate of 1,500 feet per minute. Known as Vistaliners, these aircraft were modified with oversized windows that allow excellent views for passengers.

A Cessna 185 flies along the face of the Hubbard Glacier near Yakutat, the largest tidewater glacier in North America. Its 2002 advance into nearby Gilbert Point sealed off Russell Fiord for two weeks until rising waters in the new lake broke through the ice dam. Scientists say Hubbard Glacier will continue to advance, eventually sealing off the fiord for good and turning it into "Russell Lake."

*W*hen no passengers were on board Rodger Elliott's Grumman Goose, he would occasionally practice cruising with one engine shut down and landing with the engines throttled all the way back. . . . On one engine, the Goose handles like an overloaded truck with a flat tire.

—GERRY BRUDER

Heroes of the Horizon, 1991

Kayakers load their gear into a chartered Beechcraft 18 and a de Havilland Beaver on the beach along the East Arm in Glacier Bay National Park. Air-taxi pilots need special permits to land in Alaska's national parks.

De Havilland Beaver floatplanes line the dock in Ketchikan, awaiting cruise ship passengers who will take flightseeing trips. The Beaver can carry seven passengers plus the pilot.

A Ketchikan-based Promech Air turbine Otter lands with its sight-seeing passengers at the Ketchikan waterfront. This de Havilland Otter, one of 466 built, has been converted from a 600-horsepower piston engine to a 750-horsepower turbine. The turbine conversion makes the plane faster, but also louder and less fuel-efficient.

*I*t was an unforgettable flight [in the Curtiss Model F flying boat]. Russel and Thyra passed over peak after peak. They barely skimmed the summits, to be swept downward by breathtaking downwashes in the dark, shadowed lee of each mountain and caught up by updrafts climbing the bright, windward side of the next slope.

—ROBERT MERRILL MacLEAN and SEAN ROSSITER
Flying Cold: The Adventures of Russel Merrill, Pioneer Alaskan Aviator, 1994

Two Otters and two Beavers, floatplanes large and small, decorate the Ketchikan dock, one of many places in Alaska where small planes take off and land near private homes. The buzz of aircraft engines is a common sound in Alaska, especially during the summer.

De Havilland Otters and Beavers along the downtown Juneau docks will soon be filled with cruise ship passengers, who will take flightseeing tours of the magnificent Juneau Ice Field. Otters can carry a pilot and 10 passengers; the Beaver fits seven passengers.

Two Taquan Air pilots stand beside a converted de Havilland turbine Otter watching the sunrise over Ketchikan while a de Havilland Beaver takes off from the Tongass Narrows.

SOUTHCENTRAL

Pilot Bill Kramer flies his Cessna 185 Skywagon over the Susitna River with a canoe strapped to a float. FAA regulations require pilots to have an "external load permit" to carry cargo outside of the plane. The trailing rope is used to help move and secure the plane after landing.

The region between the Alaska Range and the Gulf of Alaska is home to more than half of Alaska's population—and more than half of its registered pilots. Anchorage's Lake Hood is the largest floatplane base in the world with 1,000-plus takeoffs on the busiest summer day. Merrill Field, named for pioneer aviator Russel Merrill, covers 436 acres near downtown Anchorage and buzzes with activity at all hours in summer.

Southcentral has a milder climate than the Interior but features more rugged flying conditions in and around the Chugach Range and the Talkeetna Mountains. Southcentral also encompasses Talkeetna, the gateway to Mount McKinley for hundreds of mountain climbers each year. Air taxis out of the small Alaska town ferry hundreds of climbers to the Southeast Fork of Kahiltna Glacier each year, landing on a runway of snow and ice. Cessna 206s equipped with wheel/skis are a favorite of the Denali flyers.

Southcentral features a bit of everything Alaska has to offer for a pilot—the ocean, countless lakes, rivers large enough to use as a runway with floats, the Harding Icefield and hundreds of other glaciers, and plenty of air traffic.

41

Pilot Dave Hultquist takes off from the Sky Harbor private airstrip in south Anchorage in his de Havilland Beaver on amphibious floats. The sign warns motorists that the road intersects the airstrip.

A "float-picker" made from a modified Ford van plucks a 1949 Cessna 195 out of Lake Hood in Anchorage. The device uses a hydraulic lift to move the plane from the lake to the plane's dry dock.

*O*ne time, flying down the Copper River in the
Bellanca, Smitty ran into snow and ice. The plane
had a big sliding window on the side, which allowed the
pilot to lean over and peer out when the front window
was covered with snow and ice. Smitty leaned out, and
his hat flew off. He felt pretty sad about it because he
knew he'd never see it again. When he landed in
Cordova, he picked up the tail to pull the plane into
the hangar. There was the hat, hanging on a strut.
The only damage was a torn earflap.

—LONE E. JANSON
Mudhole Smith, Alaska Flier, 1981

On his day off from flying the
big planes, United Airlines
pilot Ward Hurlburt IV flies his
Cub Crafters "Top Cub" over
Knik Glacier in Southcentral.
The Top Cub is a new airplane
from Cub Crafters Inc. of
Yakima, Washington, that
combines most of the popular
Super Cub modifications
developed in Alaska.

Considered one of the finest examples of its kind and valued at nearly $1 million, this 1947 Grumman 47G Widgeon flies over Southcentral piloted by its owner, John Schwamm. The U.S. Coast Guard used the Grumman Widgeon to defend U.S. shorelines and rescue people at sea during World War II.

A float-equipped Piper Super Cub piloted by Doug Drum flies along the face of Excelsior Glacier in Chugach National Forest. The Super Cub, one of the most popular Alaska Bush planes, was last manufactured by the Piper company in 1983.

A de Havilland Beaver equipped with amphibious floats taxis from the owner's home onto a private airstrip in Anchorage. Many Alaska pilots consider "amphibs" an ideal landing gear. With the touch of a button, pilots are ready to land either on water or land.

Paul Claus lands his Super Cub on a glacier in Wrangell–St. Elias National Park. Few pilots attempt landing with wheels on glacier ice; skis are the landing gear of choice for most glacier pilots. Claus had stripped this plane of everything nonessential for safe flight (including the padding in the seats) to lighten the plane for short takeoffs.

49

*S*hall I go ahead or shall I turn back? The question can come on the take-off when you don't know if there is enough room. The question can come on landing when you think perhaps you had better give her the gun at the last moment and go around again. The question can be asked under a thousand different guises. But it is really always the same questions—the one Hamlet couldn't answer. Unfortunate, indecisive Hamlet would not have made a good flyer.

—CONSTANCE and HARMON HELMERICKS
The Flight of the Arctic Tern, 1952

A pair of de Havilland Beavers on floats wait for softer water on the shore of Lake Hood in January. The Canadian-built aircraft was a dependable workhorse during WW II. Today, Beavers are popular with Alaska lodge and air-taxi operators because of their large payloads and low maintenance costs. The last series of Beavers was built in the 1950s.

A de Havilland turbine Otter from K2 Aviation in Talkeetna flies over the Alaska Range on its way to taxi mountaineers to a glacier. This Otter is modified with a 500-horsepower turbine engine that dramatically increases the takeoff, climb, and cruise performance when compared to the older, heavier piston engine.

A 2002 Cub Crafters Top Cub hangs from a forklift as Anchorage AP (airframe and power plant) mechanic Scott Luce installs amphibious floats for the owner. The ritual of changing gear is big business in Alaska as most pilots change from tires or skis to floats at least twice a year.

I *remember one lady who convinced me to put a public*
address system in my plane. I had turned in my seat
occasionally to describe points of interest to my passengers.
As I turned yet again to make a comment, this lady
shouted: "Never mind, young man! Turn around and
watch where we're going!"

Anyway, a PA system was overdue.

—LOWELL THOMAS JR., *Bush Pilots of Alaska*, 1989

Super Cub pilot Sam Maxwell
fishes on a secluded lake with
Mount McKinley as a backdrop.
The white "belly tank" holds a
small amount of baggage as
well as extra fuel, extending
the range of the Cub.

A Cessna 185 sits in its parking spot on Finger Lake as Aaron Burmeister drives his team on the Iditarod Trail. An increasing number of tourists are following the annual Iditarod Trail Sled Dog Race by small plane. In winter, pilots often use an insulated engine cover with a catalytic heater inside to keep the engine oil warm overnight.

Volunteers load pre-weighed bags of musher's food and gear into "Iditarod Air Force" pilot Dr. Bill Mayer's Cessna 185. The Iditarod Air Force is a group of volunteer pilots who ferry people, supplies, and dogs to more than 20 remote checkpoints along the race route each March.

THE ARCTIC

The Arctic is a vast land of mountains and coastal plain north of the Arctic Circle, an imaginary line at 66.5 degrees north latitude. Within this mostly treeless region lies the state's northernmost mountain range, the Brooks, along with the Prudhoe Bay oilfield, and the Arctic National Wildlife Refuge.

Like no other area in Alaska, the Arctic resembles the region that once challenged pioneer flyers like Ben Eielson and Noel Wien. Because the area is so sparsely populated, pilots have few places to call for weather reports, and navigational aids are absent in large patches of the Arctic.

Landmarks can be hard to find in the Arctic, especially on the flats of the northern coast, where lakes riddle the surface like holes in Swiss cheese. The northern coast, where the Arctic landmass meets the Beaufort Sea, is often shrouded in fog, sometimes grounding pilots for days. The Brooks Range is a lovely barrier of sub-10,000-foot peaks that separate Alaska's North Slope from the Interior. Northbound pilots use caution, knowing that they could be met by dense clouds on one side despite nice weather on the other.

As the sun filters through a cloud layer, it casts a halo on the shadow of a Cessna 206. Also known as a "glory," this effect is caused by sunlight reflecting off water droplets in clouds. Glories require two things: the seer must be looking directly away from the sun, and water droplets, here provided by the clouds, must be present.

*J*ules Thibidoux was able to deliver the diesel with his rickety Stinson Voyager 108, beating out the operators with Super Cubs and the like, by concocting the technique of landing his wheel plane several yards short of the shoreline and rolling up on the hardpan from the water on momentum and with some gunning. Taking off was easy without the load of fuel.

—JOE RYCHETNIK, *Alaska's Sky Follies*, 1995

Arctic guide/pilot Phil Driver flies his Piper Super Cub over the arctic coast. This Super Cub has 30-inch tundra tires, which allow Driver to land on gravel bars, tundra, and other backcountry airstrips.

A Citabria gets on step for takeoff. The Citabria, introduced in 1964 by the Bellanca company, is the first aircraft certified in the U.S. for aerobatic flight. Citabria is "airbatic" spelled backwards.

Passengers disembark from a de Havilland Beaver and Citabria on the shore of an unnamed lake in Gates of the Arctic National Park. Floatplanes like these allow easy access to the wilds of Alaska with gear, weeks of food, inflatable boats, and other off-trail necessities.

Y ou worked with the airplanes, checking out every part of them until you knew every part inside and out. You repaired them with frozen-tipped fingers when the metal burned your bare skin like hot iron at 40 below zero; you spent more than you could afford on their upkeep; when the storms blew, you couldn't sleep until you had walked down to see how the airplane was riding the storm. You looked after it as if your life depended upon it because it did, and then when the going was rough, the chips were down, and it had given its all, there was still a little extra left under full landing flaps to lift your skis above the waves and set you safely on shore.

—BUD HELMERICKS, *The Last of the Bush Pilots*, 1969

A canoeist heads for a pickup in a Citabria on Selby Lake in the Brooks Range. The mountains are the defining geographic feature between the Interior and the Arctic, and each region poses unique challenges in climate and terrain.

A Maule waits out ground fog at a moose-hunting camp near McGrath. B. D. Maule invented the fabric-covered aircraft in the late 1950s. He envisioned the need for a four-seat aircraft rugged enough for terrain like Alaska's. His design evolved as a high-wing monoplane tail-dragger with a welded steel tube truss fuselage, metal spar wing, short-field takeoff and landing characteristics, and good range and speed.

John Norris flies his Cessna 180 over mountains near Nome. Many aircraft owners modify their planes to increase performance. This aircraft has custom wingtips that extend an extra 18 inches. The added length provides enough lift to carry 300 additional pounds.

WESTERN ALASKA

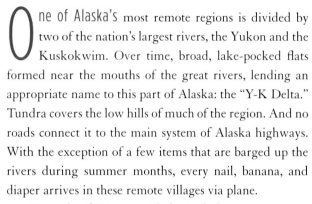

O ne of Alaska's most remote regions is divided by two of the nation's largest rivers, the Yukon and the Kuskokwim. Over time, broad, lake-pocked flats formed near the mouths of the great rivers, lending an appropriate name to this part of Alaska: the "Y-K Delta." Tundra covers the low hills of much of the region. And no roads connect it to the main system of Alaska highways. With the exception of a few items that are barged up the rivers during summer months, every nail, banana, and diaper arrives in these remote villages via plane.

Hazards of Western Alaska include strong, unpredictable winds that often result in ground blizzards, a phenomenon in which winds whip snow into a blur at ground level when blue sky remains above. Other weather challenges include frequent bouts of low clouds, rapidly changing weather, and a lack of emergency landing areas.

Southwestern Alaska, including the Alaska Peninsula and the Aleutian Islands, is a notoriously poor flying area due to weather systems that travel west to east. Common features of flying in this region are low clouds, poor visibility and high winds, coupled with few weather-reporting stations.

A Cessna 185 climbs after taking off from Naknek Lake in Katmai National Park.

A Super Cub gets a free ride along the Naknek River on the
Alaska Peninsula after the pilot ran out of fuel. He was forced
to land in a spot that was too short for takeoff, but found
a way out of his predicament.

Tourists arriving in a Cessna 206 at Naknek Lake in Katmai National Park have the company of brown bears feeding on salmon. The Cessna 206, a six-passenger plane, is manufactured with nose, or "tricycle" gear, which limits its use while on tires to smooth airstrips and paved airports. Floats are a common modification.

*T*he plane became no warmer inside but continued to get colder if anything, the winds tearing through the fabric in spite of heaters. Radio reports coming in from the trading post of Flat said that there was a 70-mile ground wind there, so we couldn't land. We battled our way over to McGrath on the upper Kuskokwim and there stayed the night at a construction camp for men who were shortly to be sent from the Aleutians.

—CONSTANCE HELMERICKS, *We Live in Alaska*, 1944

A Grumman Goose amphibious plane taxis to shore on Naknek Lake in Katmai National Park. The 10-passenger Goose was first manufactured in 1937 for the civilian marketplace and was known for its efficiency and reliability. Grumman stopped building the Goose in 1945.

Dogs gather around an Iditarod Air Force pilot's Cessna 180 for a free ride home. The pilot has modified this 180 with an air-restrictor plate over the front cowling, which retains more engine heat during the winter. He has also applied duct tape to the air cleaner to prevent the gas mixture from becoming too lean.

A Cessna 180 flies over the tundra in Western Alaska. Clyde Cessna was a pioneer in designing a monoplane with a full cantilever wing (without supporting struts or braces), and his Wichita-based aircraft company launched the Cessna All Purpose on August 13, 1927.

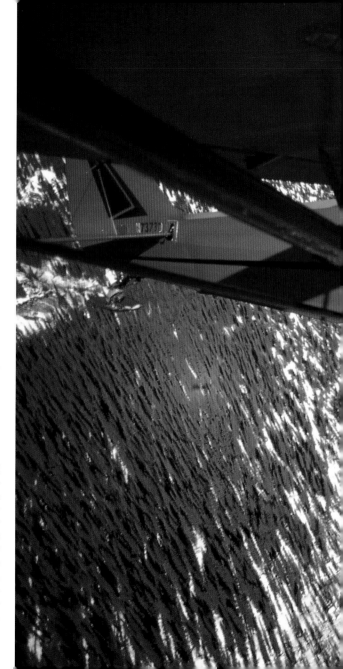

On June 19, 1927, Merrill moored Anchorage No. 1 [a Travel Air Model CW biplane] in the mouth of the Alagnak River in front of the cannery. By the next morning a steady 70 mile-an-hour gale blew out of the northeast. . . . One sudden blast caught the airplane sideways, lifted the windward wings, and flipped Anchorage No. 1 over on its back in the middle of the river. There the plane wallowed, upside down, with the tide coming in and gale-driven waves pounding its belly. Merrill could do nothing.

—ROBERT MERRILL MacLEAN and SEAN ROSSITER
Flying Cold: The Adventures of Russel Merrill, Pioneer Alaskan Aviator, 1994

Super Cub pilot Sam Maxwell maneuvers his plane so a back-seat photographer can focus on a dog team below. The Super Cub is ideal for photography because of its slow stalling speed, about 35–40 miles per hour. Straight skis are a favorite of many Alaska pilots in winter, and airports accommodate this landing gear by leaving some landing strips unplowed.

The tracks of a Cessna 185 on skis leave grooves on the surface of Little Lake Clark in Western Alaska.

Two de Havilland Beaver floatplanes face the twilight on the Agulowok River in Wood-Tikchik State Park.

A Cessna 185 functions as a kennel when a volunteer pilot of the Iditarod Air Force transports sick or tired dogs that have been dropped from the race.

Cover photos—Front: A Piper Super Cub on the Knik River. (Photo by Jeff Schultz) *Back cover, clockwise from top:* A de Havilland Otter in the Alaska Range. (Photo by Jeff Schultz) A rare Grumman Widgeon. (Photo by Jim Oltersdorf) An Otter on floats, Tongass Narrows. (Photo by Mark Kelley) *Title page photo:* An Aeronca Champ on wheels rests on frozen Lake George near Knik Glacier in Southcentral.

Library of Congress Cataloging-in-Publication Data

Rozell, Ned, 1963-
    Alaska's bush planes / text by Ned Rozell ; foreword by Harmon "Bud" Helmericks.
        p. cm.
    ISBN 0-88240-586-1 (hardbound : alk. paper)
    1. Private planes—Alaska—Pictorial works. 2. Bush flying—Alaska. I. Title.
TL685.1.R69 2004
629.133'340422'09798022—dc22   2003026373

ALASKA NORTHWEST BOOKS®
An imprint of Graphic Arts Center Publishing Company
P.O. Box 10306, Portland, Oregon 97296-0306
503-226-2402; www.gacpc.com

President: Charles M. Hopkins
Associate Publisher: Douglas A. Pfeiffer
Editorial Staff: Timothy W. Frew, Kathy Howard, Jean Andrews, Jean Bond-Slaughter
Production Staff: Richard L. Owsiany, Susan Dupere
Editor: Tricia Stinson Brown
Design, cover: Elizabeth Watson and Laura Shaw Design; interior: Laura Shaw Design
Cover photos represented by Alaska Stock Images
Map: Gray Mouse Graphics

Printed in China

Photography credits—*Front cover* and *Foreword*, page 5: Jeff Schultz. *Introduction*, page 7: Anchorage Museum of History & Art; page 9: Anchorage Museum of History & Art. *The Interior*: pages 10-13: Jeff Schultz; pages 14–15: Patrick Endres; page 16: Jeff Schultz; page 17: Eberhard Brunner; page 18: Patrick Endres; page 19: Chris Arend; pages 20–23: Eberhard Brunner. *Southeast*: pages 24–25: Mark Kelley; pages 26–30: Chip Porter; page 31: David Job; pages 32–33: Mark Kelley; page 34: Clark Mishler; page 35: Chip Porter; pages 36–37: Clark Mishler; page 38: Mark Kelley; page 39: Chip Porter. *Southcentral*: pages 40–45: Jeff Schultz; page 46: Jim Oltersdorf; page 47: Calvin Hall; page 48: Jeff Schultz; page 49: Tom Evans; pages 50–51: Eberhard Brunner; pages 52–57: Jeff Schultz. *The Arctic*: pages 58–59: Calvin Hall; pages 60–61: Eberhard Brunner; page 62: Chris Arend; pages 63–65: Arend-Pinderton; page 66: Eberhard Brunner; page 67: Jeff Schultz. *Western Alaska*: pages 68–69: Gary Schultz; page 70: Mark Emery; page 71: Johnny Johnson; pages 72–73: Diana Proemm; page 74: Jeff Schultz; page 75: Chris Arend; pages 76–77: Jeff Schultz; page 78: Jim Oltersdorf; page 79: Dan Oberlatz; page 80: Jeff Schultz. *Back cover*, clockwise from top: Jeff Schultz, Jim Oltersdorf, Mark Kelley.